I0504561

The ABC's of Startups

A Focus Guide for Business Founders

BY DAKOTA MACK

The ABC's of Startups: A Focus Guide for Business Founders

Start small,

start confident,

start knowledgeable,

start NOW!

Dakota Mack

Co-Founder & CEO

CONTENTS

Acknowledgments

I'll be the first to say that being a founder is not for the weak and when you do feel this unbearable world of Startup life on your back, you need people in your corner.

My deepest appreciation to my 'corner':

Erma, that sparked the importance of education and personal growth at an early age. Thank you for a lifetime of inspiration and encouragement that you bestowed on me.

LaTonia, that raised me and ensured I was on the right track at all times.

Terry and Minor, passionate educators that shared not only their love for education but their skills. More mentors like you are needed.

Sam Houston State University for their oppunities for personal and educational growth. For fostering my future enndeavors.

Family, Friends, Sorority sisters, co-workers, and colleagues thank you for your continued support and prayers.

....And YOU for taking the first step in launaching a new lifestyle and following your dreams. That's a huge step.

Message to Founders

Congratulations on embarking on the exciting journey of starting your own business! In this ever-evolving world of entrepreneurship, it's crucial to have a solid foundation and a clear understanding of the key principles and strategies that drive successful startups. "The ABC's of Startups" is a comprehensive guide designed to equip business founders like you with the essential knowledge and tools to navigate the challenges and maximize the opportunities that lie ahead. Let's dive in!

A IS FOR AMBITION

- Defining your vision: Setting audacious yet attainable goals
- Embracing your passion: Building a business around what you love
- Cultivating determination and resilience: Overcoming obstacles on your entrepreneurial journey

Embarking on the entrepreneurial journey is a bold and exhilarating endeavor. To thrive in this competitive landscape, business founders must possess the ability to set audacious yet attainable goals, build a business around their passion, and overcome obstacles along the way. This paper will delve into the significance of these three key aspects and highlight their role in driving entrepreneurial success.

Setting Audacious Yet Attainable Goals: Setting ambitious goals is a vital driver of entrepreneurial success. Audacity fuels innovation, pushes boundaries, and inspires others to believe in your vision. However, it is equally important to ensure that these goals remain attainable. By breaking down larger objectives into smaller, actionable steps, entrepreneurs can create a roadmap that not only challenges them but also provides a clear path towards achieving their aspirations. Setting specific, measurable, achievable, relevant, and time-bound (SMART) goals encourages focus, motivation, and a sense of purpose.

Building a Business Around Passion: Passion serves as the foundation for entrepreneurial success. When you build a business around what you love, your enthusiasm becomes infectious, driving you to go above and beyond to deliver exceptional results. Passion fuels resilience, allowing entrepreneurs to weather the storms and persevere during challenging times. By aligning your business with your interests and values, you create a purpose-driven venture that resonates with both you and your target audience, increasing the chances of sustainable growth and customer loyalty.

Overcoming Obstacles on the Entrepreneurial Journey: Obstacles are an inevitable part of the entrepreneurial journey. From financial constraints to market competition and unexpected setbacks, entrepreneurs face numerous challenges. However, it is the ability to overcome these obstacles that separates successful ventures from those that falter. Entrepreneurs must cultivate a mindset of resilience, viewing obstacles as opportunities for growth and learning. By embracing a problem-solving approach, seeking creative solutions, and leveraging the support of mentors or networks, entrepreneurs can navigate hurdles and emerge stronger than before.

B IS FOR BUSINESS PLAN

- The importance of a well-crafted business plan
- Key components of a business plan: Mission statement, market analysis, competitive analysis, marketing strategy, financial projections, and more
- How to create a compelling executive summary that captures investors' attention

A well-crafted business plan is a foundational document for any startup or business endeavor. It serves as a roadmap that outlines the company's mission, vision, goals, and strategies for achieving success. Here are some key reasons why a well-crafted business plan is crucial:

1. Clarity and Direction: A business plan provides clarity on the business's purpose, target market, and competitive landscape. It helps founders articulate their ideas and establish a clear direction for the company, guiding decision-making and resource allocation.

2. Strategy and Decision Making: By thoroughly researching and analyzing the market, competition, and customer needs, a business plan enables founders to develop effective strategies and make informed decisions. It helps identify potential risks, challenges, and opportunities, allowing for proactive planning and mitigation.

3. Funding and Investment: Investors and lenders often

require a comprehensive business plan to evaluate the viability and potential of a startup. A well-crafted plan demonstrates the founders' understanding of the market, industry trends, and revenue projections, increasing the chances of securing funding or investment.

Key Components of a Business Plan

A business plan typically consists of several key components, each serving a specific purpose in conveying the startup's vision and strategy. The essential components include:

1. Executive Summary: A concise overview of the business plan, highlighting key points and capturing the attention of potential investors or stakeholders.

2. Company Description: Detailed information about the company's history, mission, values, legal structure, and unique selling proposition.

3. Market Analysis: A comprehensive assessment of the target market, industry trends, customer needs, and competitive landscape.

4. Product or Service Offering: Detailed descriptions of the products or services offered, including features, benefits, and potential intellectual property considerations.

5. Marketing and Sales Strategy: A strategic plan for reaching the target market, acquiring customers, and positioning the brand effectively.

6. Organization and Management: An overview of the company's organizational structure, key personnel, and their roles and responsibilities.

7. Financial Projections: Detailed financial forecasts, including income statements, balance sheets, cash flow statements, and key financial ratios.

Creating a Compelling Executive Summary

The executive summary is a critical section of the business plan, as it is often the first part investors and stakeholders read. To create a compelling executive summary that captures their attention, consider the following points:

1. Conciseness: Keep the summary concise and focused, highlighting the most critical aspects of the business plan. Aim for a clear and compelling overview within one to two pages.

2. Key Highlights: Include the most significant achievements, unique aspects of the business, and key value propositions that differentiate your company from competitors.

3. Market Opportunity: Clearly articulate the market opportunity, the problem your product or service solves, and the target market size and potential growth.

4. Business Model: Provide a brief explanation of your business model and how you generate revenue.

5. Financial Overview: Summarize the financial projections and potential return on investment for investors.

6. Call to Action: Conclude the executive summary with a clear call to action, inviting investors to explore the full business plan or arrange a meeting.

Remember, the executive summary should be engaging and compelling, enticing investors to delve further into the business plan and consider investing in your venture

C IS FOR CUSTOMERS

- Identifying your target market: Conducting market research and understanding customer needs
- Crafting a value proposition: Differentiating your business from competitors
- Implementing customer-centric strategies: Acquiring, retaining, and delighting customers

In today's highly competitive business landscape, understanding your target market, crafting a compelling value proposition, and implementing customer-centric strategies are essential for sustainable success. This paper explores these key elements and highlights their significance in building customer relationships and driving business growth.

Identifying Your Target Market:

Identifying your target market is a fundamental step in developing a successful business. It involves understanding the specific demographic, psychographic, and behavioral characteristics of your ideal customers. Thorough market research, surveys, and data analysis can help uncover valuable insights into customer needs, preferences, and pain points. By segmenting your market and creating buyer personas, you can tailor your products, messaging, and marketing efforts to resonate with your target audience, increasing the chances of customer acquisition and retention.

Crafting a Value Proposition:

A value proposition is a concise statement that articulates the unique value your product or service offers to customers. It should clearly communicate the benefits, solutions, and competitive advantages your business brings to the table. Crafting a compelling value proposition involves identifying the key pain points of your target market and addressing them directly. By focusing on what sets your business apart, whether it's innovation, affordability, convenience, or superior customer service, you can differentiate yourself from competitors and capture the attention of your audience.

Implementing Customer-Centric Strategies:

Once you have identified your target market and crafted a compelling value proposition, implementing customer-centric strategies is crucial for long-term success. Putting the customer at the center of your business involves building relationships, delivering exceptional experiences, and continuously adapting to their evolving needs. This can be achieved through personalized marketing campaigns, efficient customer service, and gathering feedback to improve products and services. By listening to your customers, valuing their feedback, and demonstrating genuine care, you can cultivate loyalty, advocacy, and repeat business.

D IS FOR DELEGATION

- Assembling a winning team: Hiring the right people with complementary skills
- Overcoming delegation challenges
- Effective leadership and communication: Inspiring and motivating your team

One of the critical factors in the success of any business is the strength of its team. Assembling a winning team requires careful selection, effective delegation, and strong leadership. However, delegation can often pose challenges for business leaders. In this article, we will explore the importance of assembling a winning team, the common hurdles faced in delegation, and strategies for effective leadership and communication to overcome these challenges.

1. Assembling a Winning Team: Building a successful team begins with hiring the right individuals who possess the skills, experience, and cultural fit necessary for your organization. Look beyond qualifications and consider factors such as attitude, passion, and teamwork capabilities. A diverse team with complementary strengths can foster creativity and innovation.

2. Overcoming Delegation Challenges: Delegating tasks and responsibilities can be a daunting process for leaders. The fear of losing control or the belief that one can do tasks better can hinder effective delegation. To overcome these challenges:

a) Trust and Empowerment: Develop a culture of trust within the team by clearly defining roles and responsibilities. Empower team members with the authority to make decisions and take ownership of their tasks. Encourage open dialogue, listen to their ideas, and provide guidance when needed.

b) Effective Communication: Establish a clear line of communication with team members. Set expectations, goals, and deadlines clearly, ensuring that everyone understands their responsibilities. Encourage open and honest communication, where team members can ask questions, seek clarification, and provide feedback.

c) Training and Development: Invest in the professional growth of your team members. Provide training opportunities to enhance their skills, encourage cross-functional learning, and promote personal development. This not only builds their confidence but also equips them with the tools needed to excel in their delegated tasks.

3. Effective Leadership and Communication: Leadership plays a vital role in creating a conducive environment for effective delegation. Employ the following strategies to foster strong leadership and communication:

a) Lead by Example: Set high standards for yourself and demonstrate the behavior and work ethic you expect from your team. Show integrity, dedication, and a commitment to excellence. This inspires trust and motivates team members to follow suit.

b) Clear Communication Channels: Establish regular and open lines of communication. Encourage face-to-face interactions, team meetings, and one-on-one sessions. Use various communication tools and platforms to keep everyone informed and engaged. Be approachable and available to address concerns or questions.

c) Provide Feedback and Recognition: Offer constructive feedback to help team members improve and grow. Acknowledge their accomplishments and provide recognition for their hard work and contributions. Celebrate milestones and successes collectively to foster a positive team culture.

d) Encourage Collaboration: Promote a collaborative environment where ideas can be shared freely. Encourage teamwork, cross-functional collaboration, and knowledge sharing. Foster an inclusive culture where every team member feels valued and heard.

E IS FOR EXECUTION

- Turning ideas into action: Developing an execution plan
- Managing resources and timelines
- Iterative approach: Embracing feedback and adapting to market dynamics

Turning Ideas into Action: Ideas are the lifeblood of any startup, but it's the execution that truly sets successful ventures apart. Turning ideas into action requires careful planning, a bias towards action, and the ability to adapt along the way. Start by breaking down your ideas into actionable steps and setting clear objectives. Create a roadmap that outlines the key milestones and tasks necessary to bring your ideas to life. This will provide a sense of direction and help you stay focused. However, it's important to strike a balance between planning and taking action. Don't get caught in analysis paralysis; instead, embrace a mindset of experimentation and learning. Iterate quickly, gather feedback, and make necessary adjustments along the way. Remember, execution is where the rubber meets the road.

Managing Resources and Timelines: Effective resource management is crucial for startups operating with limited budgets and tight timelines. Identify the resources required to execute your plans, including financial capital, human resources, technology, and physical assets. Prioritize and allocate resources based on their criticality and impact on your business objectives. Keep a close eye on your budget and cash flow, making sure to optimize spending and explore cost-effective solutions. When it comes to timelines, set realistic deadlines and create a project schedule that outlines the sequence of activities and dependencies. Regularly monitor progress and adjust timelines as needed. Effective resource and timeline management will help you stay on track and maximize the efficiency of your operations.

Iterative Approach: In the fast-paced world of startups, the iterative approach is key to success. Instead of striving for perfection from the outset, embrace a mindset of continuous improvement and iteration. Launch an initial version of your product or service, gather feedback from early adopters or customers, and use that feedback to enhance and refine your offering. By taking an iterative approach, you can quickly identify and address flaws, pivot if necessary, and adapt to changing market dynamics. This approach also enables you to test assumptions and validate your business model before scaling. Embrace failure as an opportunity to learn and iterate. Each iteration brings you closer to product-market fit and helps you build a strong foundation for long-term success.

F IS FOR FINANCING

- Understanding different sources of funding: Bootstrapping, angel investors, venture capital, crowdfunding, loans, and grants
- Preparing for investor pitches: Creating a compelling pitch deck and mastering the art of storytelling
- Financial management: Budgeting, forecasting, and tracking key metrics

Securing adequate funding is a crucial aspect of any startup's success. Understanding the different sources of funding available can significantly impact a business's growth trajectory. Whether it's bootstrapping, seeking angel investors, venture capital, crowdfunding, loans, or grants, each option comes with its own considerations and implications.

Bootstrapping involves self-funding the business using personal savings or revenue generated by the startup itself. While it provides full control, it may limit scalability and pose financial risks. Angel investors, on the other hand, can offer not just capital but also valuable guidance and networks. Venture capital firms typically invest in high-growth potential startups in exchange for equity. Crowdfunding platforms allow entrepreneurs to raise funds from a large pool of individuals, often by showcasing their products or services through compelling storytelling.

Preparing for investor pitches is a critical step in securing funding. Crafting a compelling narrative around the business can capture the attention and interest of potential investors. Storytelling allows founders to present their vision, market opportunity, and unique value proposition in a memorable and relatable manner. Effective storytelling engages investors emotionally, helping them connect with the business's purpose and potential impact.

Financial management is fundamental for startups to sustain and thrive. Budgeting, forecasting, and tracking key financial metrics are essential for understanding the company's financial health and making informed decisions. Startups should develop realistic financial projections that demonstrate a solid understanding of their market, revenue streams, and expenses. Effective financial management also includes managing cash flow, ensuring proper allocation of funds, and maintaining transparency with investors.

Furthermore, startups must establish financial controls and implement accounting systems to accurately monitor and report financial performance. Regular financial audits and assessments help identify areas for improvement and provide insights into the company's financial sustainability.

G IS FOR GROWTH

- Strategies for scaling your business: Expanding into new markets, launching new products, and optimizing operations
- Leveraging technology and innovation to drive growth
- Building strategic partnerships and collaborations

Scaling a business is an exciting but challenging endeavor. To achieve sustainable growth and expand your reach, it is essential to employ effective strategies, leverage technology and innovation, and build strategic partnerships and collaborations. These three elements play crucial roles in propelling your business forward.

When it comes to scaling your business, strategic planning is key. Start by identifying your target markets and customer segments. Develop a growth strategy that aligns with your vision and goals. This may involve penetrating new markets, diversifying your product or service offerings, or expanding geographically. Implementing efficient operational processes, streamlining supply chains, and optimizing resource allocation will also facilitate scalability.

Leveraging technology and innovation is a vital component of growth. Embrace technological advancements that align with your business model and industry. Utilize automation tools, data analytics, and artificial intelligence to enhance operational efficiency, improve customer experiences, and identify new growth opportunities. By staying abreast of emerging technologies, you can gain a competitive edge and adapt to changing market demands.

Building strategic partnerships and collaborations can be instrumental in driving growth. Seek out synergistic alliances with complementary businesses or organizations. These partnerships can open new distribution channels, access additional resources, and tap into new markets. Collaborative ventures can also foster innovation and knowledge sharing, leading to enhanced product development and a stronger competitive position.

To maximize the benefits of partnerships, establish clear objectives and align expectations. Foster trust and maintain open communication with your partners. Regularly assess the performance of collaborations and make adjustments as needed to ensure mutual success.

H IS FOR HUMAN RESOURCES

- Hiring, onboarding, and retaining top talent
- Developing effective performance management systems
- Creating a learning and development culture

In today's competitive business landscape, the success of a startup heavily relies on the talent and skills of its workforce. Hiring, onboarding, and retaining top talent are critical components for building a high-performing team. Additionally, developing effective performance management systems and creating a development culture are crucial for nurturing employee growth and optimizing their potential. This paper explores strategies to excel in these areas and create an environment conducive to attracting, engaging, and retaining exceptional talent.

Hiring, Onboarding, and Retaining Top Talent:

To attract top talent, it is essential to define clear job roles, requirements, and a compelling employee value proposition. By leveraging multiple channels, including online platforms and professional networks, startups can cast a wider net and reach qualified candidates. Implementing a thorough and rigorous selection process, including interviews, assessments, and reference checks, ensures that the right individuals are hired.

Once hired, a robust onboarding process is crucial to facilitate a smooth transition into the organization. Providing comprehensive orientation, training, and mentorship helps new hires become acclimated to the company culture, understand their roles, and build relationships with colleagues.

Retaining top talent requires a focus on employee engagement and satisfaction. Offering competitive compensation and benefits packages, providing growth opportunities, and creating a supportive work environment with open communication and recognition programs are effective strategies for enhancing employee loyalty.

Developing Effective Performance Management Systems:

Effective performance management systems involve setting clear performance expectations, providing regular feedback, and conducting performance evaluations. By defining measurable goals and objectives, employees have a clear understanding of what is expected of them. Regular feedback sessions enable constructive dialogue, coaching, and addressing any performance gaps promptly.

Performance evaluations, conducted on a regular basis, provide an opportunity to assess employee performance objectively. These evaluations can be complemented by 360-degree feedback, where input is gathered from peers, subordinates, and supervisors, allowing for a comprehensive assessment.

Creating a Development Culture:

Fostering a development culture entails promoting continuous learning and growth opportunities for employees. Offering training programs, workshops, and access to industry conferences enhances their knowledge and skills. Additionally, implementing mentorship programs and providing opportunities for job rotations and cross-functional projects cultivates a culture of personal and professional development.

Encouraging employees to set individual development goals and supporting them in achieving those goals is essential. This can be accomplished through regular performance discussions, career planning sessions, and offering resources such as online learning platforms or tuition reimbursement programs.

I IS FOR INNOVATION

- Fostering a culture of innovation within your startup
- Encouraging creativity and problem-solving
- Embracing emerging technologies and trends

Fostering a Culture of Innovation within Your Startup

In today's rapidly evolving business landscape, fostering a culture of innovation is essential for the success and sustainability of any startup. Creating an environment that encourages and nurtures innovation can drive creativity, problem-solving, and the adoption of emerging technologies and trends. Here are key points to consider when cultivating an innovative culture within your startup.

Encouraging Creativity and Problem-Solving

Creativity and problem-solving are the lifeblood of innovation. Encourage your team to think outside the box, challenge existing norms, and explore new possibilities. Create a safe space where ideas are welcomed and no concept is immediately dismissed. Foster an open and collaborative work environment that encourages brainstorming sessions, cross-functional collaboration, and diverse perspectives. Provide employees with autonomy and freedom to experiment, take risks, and learn from failures. Recognize and reward innovative thinking to reinforce the value you place on creativity and problem-solving.

Embracing Emerging Technologies and Trends

To stay ahead in a competitive market, startups must embrace emerging technologies and trends that are relevant to their industry. Encourage your team to stay informed about advancements in technology and market trends. Foster a learning culture by providing opportunities for training, attending conferences, and engaging with industry experts. Actively seek out innovative solutions and technologies that can enhance your products, services, or processes. Embrace experimentation and pilot projects to test the feasibility and potential impact of emerging technologies. Be willing to adapt and pivot quickly to leverage new opportunities presented by technological advancements.

GLOSSARY

Accelerator: A program that provides startups with mentorship, resources, and funding to accelerate their growth and development.

Angel Investor: An individual who provides financial support to startups in exchange for equity ownership.

Bootstrapping: Building a startup using personal funds or operating revenue without external investment.

Burn Rate: The rate at which a startup consumes its cash reserves to cover expenses before becoming profitable.

Business Model Canvas: A strategic tool used to visualize and analyze the key elements of a startup's business model.

Churn Rate: The rate at which customers stop using a product or service over a given period.

Convertible Note: A form of short-term debt that converts into equity at a future milestone, typically during a funding round.

Crowdfunding: Raising funds for a startup by collecting small amounts of money from a large number of individuals via online platforms.

Customer Acquisition Cost (CAC): The cost a startup incurs to acquire a new customer, including marketing and sales expenses.

Disruptive Innovation: An innovation that creates a new market by displacing established products or services.

Equity: Ownership interest in a startup, usually in the form of shares or stock options.

Exit Strategy: A plan for how startup founders and investors will realize their financial gains, such as through an acquisition or initial public offering (IPO).

Freemium: A business model that offers basic services for free but charges for advanced features or additional services.

Growth Hacking: Using unconventional marketing strategies and techniques to achieve rapid and scalable growth for a startup.

Incubator: A program or organization that provides resources and support to early-stage startups, often in exchange for equity.

Intellectual Property (IP): Legal rights to protect the intangible assets of a startup, such as patents, trademarks, and copyrights.

Lean Startup: An approach to startup development that emphasizes rapid experimentation, iterative product releases, and customer feedback.

Market Validation: The process of confirming that a startup's product or service satisfies a market need and has a potential customer base.

Minimum Viable Product (MVP): A basic version of a product with enough features to gather user feedback and validate assumptions.

Pivot: A strategic change in a startup's direction or business model in response to market feedback or changing circumstances.

Runway: The length of time a startup can sustain its operations with its available financial resources.

Scalability: The ability of a startup to handle increased demand and grow its business without compromising performance or quality.

Seed Funding: Early-stage capital provided to a startup to support its initial development and product launch.

Serial Entrepreneur: An individual who starts multiple businesses over their career, often in different industries.

Stealth Mode: A period during which a startup operates in secret, without publicizing its product or plans, to avoid competition or premature attention.

Sweat Equity: Contributing time, effort, or expertise to a startup in exchange for equity rather than monetary compensation.

Term Sheet: A non-binding document outlining the terms and conditions of an investment agreement between a startup and an investor.

Traction: Evidence of market demand and customer adoption of a startup's product or service.

Unicorn: A startup with a valuation of $1 billion or more, often achieved through rapid growth and high investor interest.

User Experience (UX): The overall experience and satisfaction of users when interacting with a startup's product or service.

Venture Capital (VC): Investment capital provided by specialized funds to startups with high growth potential in exchange for equity.

RESOURCES

- Small Business Administration (SBA): The SBA provides resources, programs, and information on starting and managing a small business. They offer assistance with business planning, loans, grants, and more. Website: www.sba.gov

- SCORE: SCORE is a nonprofit organization that offers free mentoring and counseling services to small business owners. They also provide workshops, webinars, and templates for business planning. Website: www.score.org

- U.S. Small Business Development Centers (SBDC): SBDCs provide free or low-cost consulting services to small businesses. They offer guidance on various aspects of business development, such as marketing, finance, and operations. Website: www.sba.gov/sbdc

- StartUpNation: StartUpNation is an online resource for entrepreneurs that offers articles, forums, and resources on various topics related to starting and growing a business. Website: www.startupnation.com

- Small Business Development Centers (SBDCs): SBDCs are local organizations funded by the government and universities that provide free consulting and training to small businesses. They offer guidance on business planning, market research, financing, and more. Website: www.americassbdc.org

- AngelList: AngelList is a platform connecting startups with investors, job seekers, and mentors. It offers access to startup job postings, fundraising opportunities, and a network of experienced professionals. Website: www.angel.co

- Crunchbase: Crunchbase is a comprehensive database of startup information, including funding rounds, acquisitions, and key personnel. It can be a valuable resource for market research and networking. Website: www.crunchbase.com

- Small Business Forums: Online forums, such as the Small Business Forum and Reddit's r/smallbusiness, provide platforms for entrepreneurs to ask questions, share experiences, and learn from others in the small business community.

- Small Business Legal Assistance: LegalZoom and Rocket Lawyer are online platforms that offer affordable legal services, including business formation, contract creation, and legal advice for startups. Websites: www.legalzoom.com, www.rocketlawyer.com

- Small Business Financial Tools: QuickBooks and FreshBooks are popular accounting software solutions that can help small businesses manage their finances, track expenses, and generate financial reports. Websites: www.quickbooks.intuit.com, www.freshbooks.com

- Small Business Marketing: HubSpot and Mailchimp provide marketing tools, resources, and guides for small businesses. They offer email marketing, social media management, CRM solutions, and more. Websites: www.hubspot.com, www.mailchimp.com

- Founder Institute: The Founder Institute is a global startup accelerator and launch program that helps aspiring entrepreneurs turn their ideas into successful businesses. They provide training, mentorship, and networking opportunities to early-stage startups. Website: www.fi.co

- Y Combinator: Y Combinator is one of the most prestigious startup accelerators and seed funding providers in the world. They offer a three-month program for early-stage startups, along with access to a strong network of mentors and investors. Website: www.ycombinator.com

- Startup Grind: Startup Grind is a global community of entrepreneurs that hosts events, conferences, and fireside chats with successful founders, investors, and thought leaders. It offers valuable networking opportunities and inspirational stories. Website: www.startupgrind.com

- Small Business Innovation Research (SBIR) and Small Business Technology Transfer (STTR) Programs: These U.S. government programs provide funding opportunities for small businesses engaged in research and development. They support innovative projects that have the potential for

commercialization. Website: www.sbir.gov